BLUFF YOUR WAY IN
TELEVISION

RICHARD SPENCE &
VICTOR VAN
AMERONGEN

D1547984

ℛ

Ravette London

Published by Ravette Limited
3 Glenside Estate, Star Road,
Partridge Green, Horsham,
Sussex RH13 8RA
(0403) 710392

Series Editor – Anne Tauté

Cover design – Jim Wire
Typesetting – Input Typesetting Ltd.
Origination – Acorn Litho Colour Printers Ltd.
Printing & Binding – Cox & Wyman Ltd.
Production – Oval Projects Ltd.

The Bluffer's Guides are based on
an original idea by Peter Wolfe.

For the objects on the cover, grateful thanks are due to:
Viewplan Broadcast, Indescon Court, Millharbour,
Millwall Docks, London E14 9TM

CONTENTS

After the Programme 51

Appearing on
  Television 49

Arts Programmes 41

Autocue 19

Awards 53

Background 7

Camerman (Film) 11

Camermen (Studio) 16

Children's
  Programmes 38

Current Affairs 24

Documentaries 40

Drama 27

Editing 21

Education 42

Film 10

Floor Manager 17

Game Shows 34

Global Vision 56

Great Names 43

Grips 14

Jargon 59

Light Entertainment 31

Lights 13

News 23

Outside Broadcasts 20

P.A. and V.M. 19

Presenters 17

Production 22

Programme Makers 10

Programmes 23

Ratings Game 51

Reith 50

Religion 37

Science 37

Soaps 29

Sound 12

Sport 26

Studio 14

TV Tech 54

Youth Programmes 39

THE AUTHORS

Richard Spence and Victor van Amerongen both work for a famous national broadcasting network. Under the terms of their BBC contracts they cannot say which one it is (but it's very big and impressive).

Both have been carefully selected by the organisation and groomed for the appropriate jobs. The latter finds his background in theoretical physics and electronic music invaluable in producing Current Affairs; the former draws constantly on his knowledge of Latin, Greek, philosophy and rock'n'roll drumming to make serious programmes on the Arts.

Although the formulation, preparation and dissection of television takes up most of their lives, they do have other interests. They collaborate on the composition and recording of novelty songs and other supposedly humorous ventures.

Richard Spence and Victor van Amerongen (he's Dutch, you know) are devoted to their present employer but may yet become 'independent producers'. As yet they're not that desperate.

INTRODUCTION

Everyone watches television, even if they try to tell you that they don't. Nowadays 98 per cent of homes in Britain have a television set and the average person watches some 27 hours a week. Most households spend at least a third of that time squabbling over which channel to watch, and a further 10 per cent arguing about what to record on the video. But even so it's a lot.

The only people who genuinely don't watch television are 'radio people'. They hate television. They hate it because it is pervasive, popular and gaudy. Instead they listen to the 'Home Service' or the 'Third Programme' on the 'wireless' and enjoy the feeling of intimacy derived from being part of a very small audience. They are the ones who still ramble on about Reithian values and the Dunkirk spirit.

The bluffer's position is to abjure both extremes. You should condemn the average viewer (even if you are one) for the mindless and uncritical consumption of an endless stream of televisual pap. But dismiss the radio lover as being totally out of touch; the radio's only remaining use is to give time checks and the final warning of a nuclear war.

Television is and always has been a mass of confusions, a jumble of jargon, buzz-words and contradictory programme policies of head-spinning proportions. Even the word 'television' is confused. It's a hybrid of Greek and Latin that really ought to be either 'telerama' or 'proculvision' to make any sense at all.

This confusion is compounded by the complicated nature of television. Each area has its own language, as do the several different television companies and networks. And they in turn sell their product to companies abroad who have fresh jargon, systems and symbols to baffle even the most seasoned television lexicographer.

Thus the bluffer's task is relatively simple. All you have to do is take advantage of this confusion. Learn a smattering of arcane technical terms, a soupcon of programme-maker's know-how and a rag bag of the general gossipy minutiae that make up the Wonderful World of Television. You don't have to know what much of it means, just reel it off with confidence and authority. After all that's what television executives have been doing for years.

Background

The man generally credited with inventing television was the Scot, **Logie Baird** (not to be confused with Yogi Bear, a much later exponent of the same medium). His **televisor** system, dating from 1925, used a giant spinning disc to scan someone with beams of light in an otherwise darkened room. Even then the total area scanned was only one foot square, severely restricting the potential for great dramatic performances. Not surprisingly most of Baird's subjects were wax dummies as few performers were prepared to put up with these working conditions.

You need not concern yourself unduly with Baird's ideas because by 1936 it was obvious that a rival electronic system was far better. It was developed by one **Isaac Schoenberg** – a real showstopper of a name to drop. Using his system, the **BBC** launched the world's first 'high-definition television service' from **Alexandra Palace** in north London (always referred to in the business as 'Ally Pally').

In spite of the prevailing mythology about the Golden Age of Broadcasting the service was abysmal. Point out that to become a viewer you had to live in London, that a television set cost more than a car and that although the system was high-definition, the programme content was extremely fuzzy. It is entirely appropriate that the last image seen on television before it closed down for the Second World War was that of Mickey Mouse.

When the service resumed in 1945, television was still very much something for the idle rich or the aspiring boffin. It wasn't until 1953 and the live broadcasting of The Coronation that millions of people felt the urge to have a set of their own.

Technically little changed until 1967 and the introduction to Britain of colour television. Americans may boast that they had colour several years earlier. But remind them that first is not always best; their **NTSC** system is popularly described by the acronym Never Twice the Same Colour. It's 'low definition' and they're lumbered with it.

The workings of a modern television set are of little importance. You should know that the various broadcasting systems used around the world – **PAL, NTSC, SECAM**, etc. – are totally incompatible and that the picture quality of PAL is by far the best. You should also know that TV pictures are made up from little phosphorous dots of just three colours – red, green and blue – painted on the inside of the screen at the front of a cathode ray tube. This allows you to fiddle with faulty sets and mumble with confidence about 'gun deflection' and 'tube alignment'.

Finally, never call the thing a television. You can call it a television set, but the term **receiver** has more authority. Ideally use the fashionable industry jargon: refer to anything that looks remotely like a television as a **monitor**.

You must realise too that modern television does not stand alone. The minute you switch on you are 'interfacing with the communications explosion', 'logging on to a worldwide data network' and 'entering the universe of on-line/off-line decision making'. Television is now described as **state-of-the-art**. In practical terms this means that by attaching various gizmos to your set, you can receive, process, store, compile and edit sound and vision from Russia, Australia, Scunthorpe or the Moon.

The advance of science is wonderful. Unfortunately the programmes usually aren't.

WHO MAKES TELEVISION

Television is highly labour intensive. Although it relies heavily on machines and needs them at all stages of production and transmission, it cannot programme them to make the programmes themselves, however much the final product may look like it.

What the bluffer needs to realize is that this combination of the desire for ever more sophisticated electronics and un-technically minded 'creative' production staff leads to enormous complexity. First of all, it creates the need for a large range of **technical specialists**, each one in charge of a narrowly defined aspect of hardware (jobs include Head of Image Scanning, Head of Baseband Systems and Assistant Head of Propagation). Secondly, each specialist despises all others and hides behind the prerogatives and jargon of their own little area.

Even so there does have to be some attempt at communication between these specialists as well as between specialists and bewildered production staff. So there evolves a phalanx of non-technical non-production people who manage or back up this **inter-departmental liaison** with titles like Manager, Controlled Loans (Bibliographic Services), Head of Consultancy, Deputy Head of Continuous Services and Realisations Manager. These managers maintain their power in the time honoured way by having meetings, sending each other memos and creating more tiers of management below them. They know a bit about other people's jobs but not much about their own.

So you must realise that in television few people are concerned with actually making programmes; many, many more are paid a lot of money to prevent them being made.

The other favourite tactic is to pass producers from one so-called **service department** to another in a never ending cycle until despair takes hold and the project is abandoned.

Programme Makers

Clearly, making programmes is difficult. So any serious bluffer needs to know the outline process of production and roughly who does what to be convincingly expert or critical. Wincing at a crass error on the screen is so much easier if you know who's immediately responsible. It's a splendid management technique. It helps deflect attention from those who are really to blame.

Programmes can be recorded on film at a location or on videotape in the studio or at an outside broadcast (**O.B**. as you should always call it). You must also be aware that film technicians refer to themselves as 'craft' while their studio/O.B. counterparts are 'engineering'. The two disciplines distrust each other fundamentally. They are only united in their wariness of anyone from '**production**'.

Film

When television began, its film-making technicians were taken from the feature film industry. TV film crews still carry with them a portion of this reflected cowboy glamour. Film crews get to travel everywhere and consequently know everything. After a brief meeting they can tell anyone in any part of the globe how they ought to run their life if they had any sense. They know the best hotels and restaurants throughout the world and what you should order in each one. Wherever they go, wherever anyone takes them, they've always been somewhere more interesting and with a better director.

For example: there's a shoot for current affairs in Catford and it's raining. The cameraman and his assistant are at the meeting place (the R.V.) in the camera car. The drenched director approaches. Note that the cameraman will always roll down the electric window of his Volvo and talk noisily to his assistant about last week's brilliant drama in Kenya for at least fifteen seconds before acknowledging today's damp representative of Production.

Film crews vary in size depending on the type of programme and union agreements. A drama, especially if it has nude scenes, finds that its crew needs to be enormous. Including costume, make-up, chippies (carpenters), design, transport and general scenic operatives, the number rises upwards of sixty. In war zones a typical crew size is two men. And in America some low-budget news stations now use a single operator as cameraman, sound recordist and reporter.

All the bluffer needs to be familiar with is the normal nucleus:

The Cameraman

These are usually still men though you should know that **cameraman** is legally a 'customary description' and there are now women cameramen, however little they may like the title. The cameraman runs the crew and, if possible, the director. All cameramen have done every shot before and will try to show you the tripod marks where they set up the camera for the same shot back in 1967. They like to refer to themselves as **lighting cameramen** as they also use lights.

There is a good deal of one-upmanship between cameramen about lighting. The one with the most smoke guns and big bits of reflecting polystyrene usually wins.

The Assistant Cameraman

This is the individual who hopes one day to be a cameraman but now has to be content with hauling the tripod about and, as a treat, driving the camera car. He spends a lot of time with his arms in a piece of black cloth doing something that looks disgusting. In fact he is **in the bag**, loading rolls of film into magazines out of the light. The rest of the time is spent being a double act with the cameraman. Discussing hotels as essential daylight fades is a speciality. Assistant cameramen also:

a) **pull focus** – change the focus of the lens during a shot

b) clap the clapperboard to identify the shot.

On a drama they may split these functions with a more menial **clapper-loader**.

Sound

Sound recordists have a bizarre and warped perspective on the world. They wear headphones and wave about a highly sensitive directional microphone called a **gun mike** that looks like a large grey salami. They can hear incredibly clearly all the sounds coming from the direction in which their mike is pointed but nothing else. So they get abnormally twitchy about

12

extraneous noise that only they can hear. 'We'll have to do that again', they say, 'There was an ant scratching'.

On the other hand you can walk up and talk right into a sound recordist's face without getting any response. Only if the salami is pointing your way does anything register.

Sound recordists often seem woefully lonely. In television, people are concerned with pictures. Everyone huddles around the cameraman working out the great sequence of shots. Meanwhile sound stands silent some distance away, ignored but eavesdropping on a small private world.

Lights

Lighting electricians are always known as **sparks**. Again they're almost always men. Sparks set up, move and switch on the lights according to the cameraman's instruction. If it's a large set-up, like a drama, several sparks work under the supervision of a **gaffer**.

If the crew has a wide-boy (and it usually does) it'll be the spark. Sparks specialise in two things – overtime and obfuscation. Every spark is master of every obscure regulation pertaining to meal-breaks, extra hours and penalty payments, and much spare time (chargeable) is spent filling in the appropriate sheets. And sparks' talk is a language all of its own. There is endless reference to **blondes**, **red-heads** and **pups**: not girl-friends and dogs (although they may be) but different types of lamp. They also have a good line in rhyming slang so that 'Giving it a lemon on the barnet' means flashing light on someone's hair. The cameraman understands, the director's in the dark; mission accomplished.

Grips

The **grip** 'dollies the camera when it needs to track' (learn this phrase and use it as often as possible). In other words he mounts the camera on a wheeled vehicle and pushes it along. The wheeled vehicle is called **the dolly** and **the track** is both the technical term for the movement of the camera and the metal rail along which the dolly moves. He also operates **jibs** and **cranes** when the camera needs to go up and down.

All grips are called either Nobby or Tex. Even more than the rest of the crew, the seasoned grip knows everything and is careful to tell the director. Grips specialise in legendary tales of terrific tracks and great jib movements they have known, which they like to pause and tell when everyone else is struggling over a difficult shot.

Studio

If film crews are world-roaming individualists (they aren't but they think they are) studio crews are the solid, reliable stay-at-home type. The essential thing to know is that the philosophy of the studio is entirely different from that of film. People come *to* the studio crew rather than the studio crew going to the people.

Studios are cavernously functional and depressingly like aircraft hangars. The idea is that they can be transformed into places of breathtaking beauty or futurist fantasy by the simple expedient of wheeling in a cardboard and plywood **set**. Be aware that these sets are only ever partial: what you see is all there is. So the actor sitting by that cosy fire in a highland croft is actually sitting between two flimsy wooden walls in an electronic barn in a dingy urban suburb. There's no ceiling and even the fire is false.

Most studios contain not one, but four or five cameras. These are large, electronic, have their own wheeled pedestal (no loquacious grips here) and are left permanently switched on. The output of the cameras is seen simultaneously on monitors in the studio control room (**the gallery**) where the director holds sway. Shots from different cameras are recorded in sequence on videotape somewhere else in the building. So everyone is separated: the crew on the studio floor, sound, lights and the director in their own little areas of the production suite upstairs and videotape far away in the basement.

Studio Director
All this gives the studio director a major advantage: there's no need to be polite to anyone. Unlike film directors who are down amongst their crew and have to be grovellingly polite, studio directors can see from the gallery monitors what everyone is doing and can order them around at long distance. These imperious messages are conveyed by the headphone radio system known inappropriately as '**talkback**'.

Note that studio directors are actually trained not to say please to anyone (though they're supposed to say thank you after the programme) and that the glitzy electronic layout of the gallery encourages megalomania.

Scenic Operatives
Like film drama locations, studios have their complement of assorted workers. Since sets are put in overnight before engineering and production staff arrive, most of these people are never seen (especially when

needed). Others are trying to avoid the director's nagging voice and there's always that handful using spare moments (chargeable) for filling in their overtime sheets. The bluffer can ignore these people (they're well used to it) and concentrate on the main protagonists.

Cameramen

Like all engineering functions, studio cameramen have been reduced to digits. The director never refers to them by name, only by the number of the camera they happen to be operating that day ('O.K. Three, track right; Four, give me a wide shot').

They have the additional frustration of never being able to see a sequence of shots, let alone the whole programme. Their viewfinder only shows them the output of their own camera, and then only in black-and-white. They spend a large amount of time lumbering around the studio floor trying to keep out of each other's way.

Unlike film cameramen, studio cameramen have to keep quiet. They can't even speak when spoken to; if they want to say anything to the director they have to press a special '**reverse talkback**' button and wait for permission to speak. Even then it is not unknown for directors to switch this circuit off to avoid any challenge to their autocracy.

The final insult for the studio cameraman is to have to stand around all day listening to orders without getting more than one or two shots to do. Alternatively, especially in sport or current affairs, they have to hold the same shot for hours on end.

In BBC Television News, cameramen have been replaced by robots.

Floor Manager

This is the director's mouthpiece on the studio floor. Because the director's edicts can only be heard by those wearing **cans** (headphones), the **F.M.** has to convey instructions to actors, presenters and anyone else in the firing line. A substantial part of a good F.M.'s job is tact. Even when the talkback is blue with insults, the floor manager is firm but polite. Thus director's instruction to 'Get that fat idiot to put his bum on the ****ing chair!' would be translated as 'Could you sit here please?'

During the transmission of a live programme, even the floor manager must keep quiet. So a complicated code of hand signals is used to pass on instructions. These include **the fifteen second wind**, a sort of circular flailing action which indicates to a presenter that an interview must be concluded. If the presenter fails, more frantic signals such as **the hard wind** and **the cut-throat** translate cries of 'Shut up, you fool' from the director's chair.

There are two junior floor managers to order around, the **Assistant Floor Manager** and the equally imaginatively titled **Floor Assistant**. Their main job is help preseve the F.M.'s sanity.

Presenters

The first thing to know is that **presenters** aren't really programme makers however much they might like to think that they are.

They may look into the camera with an air of concerned sincerity and pronounce on the affairs of the world with seeming authority. In fact all they are doing is reading words written by someone else earning a fraction of their fee. Note that experienced presenters move their heads around to emphasise what they say. This is an old ploy to stop viewers noticing their eyes swivelling desperately as they read the Autocue (*q.v.*).

The main function of the presenter is give a programme a spurious illusion of stability. Even if things are in a total state of hysteria and chaos in the gallery and out of shot, presenters must carry on blandly reciting the inanities projected before them, disguising their fear that even Autocue may fail.

Their other task is to make everything appear **seamless**. Although most **magazine** programmes are simply a rag bag of ill-assorted odds and ends thrown together at the last moment, the presenter must give the impression that all is in logical sequence. To do this they employ the **ad lib back ref.**, the verbal equivalent of an amateur magician's sleight of hand. These 'links' are easy for bluffers to spot and parody.

Example: An item about sheep shearing precedes a feature on Indian food.

THE PRESENTER: 'Well, from one type of flock to another. Flock wallpaper that is. And where are you most likely to see it? Over a steaming mutton vindaloo in your friendly local Tandoori restaurant. From the Taj Mahal, Kettering, we bring you a spicy report . . .'

Finally, look out for the favourite ruse of television sport, the **visual run cue**. Programmes like *Grandstand* are live and not worth scripting. So the presenter will be told by the producer to link outside broadcast events in their own words. But how is the director to know when the presenter has finished their **rabbit**? Easy. During the first item a bit of body language is selected that will look to the viewers like innocuous fidgeting but indicates to the director that the presenter is about to **wind up** and the next item should finally be run. It's a time-honoured technique. When David Coleman pulls his earlobe, Venezualan frog-jousting is just five seconds away.

Autocue
Autocue or **Teleprompt** are the systems invented so that presenters don't have to learn their lines.

The **Autocue operator** sits within shouting distance across the studio floor. She (usually it is a she) has already transcribed the script onto long rolls of lavatory-like paper and feeds these through a machine which is linked to the projector on the camera as the presenter reads.

Presenters rely on Autocue operators like a child does its mother and have recurrent nightmares about machine failure. Without autocue most presenters are left gulping like goldfish.

P.A. and V.M.
The **Production Assistant** and **Vision Mixer** have the thankless task of sitting either side of the director in the studio gallery.

P.A.s are trained to time all the sections of the programme and prevent it over- or under-running. They also spend a lot of time counting backwards to cue things to happen.

V.M.s are the people who actually press the buttons that '**cut up**' shots from the various cameras. They also operate the **effects bank** which create complicated visuals like **coloured-edged wipes** or **luminance key insertions** or **overlay with slide file**. Mention these when something vaguely clever happens on your screen and cite their failure when things go wrong.

The real job of both Production Assistant and Vision Mixer is to bail directors, out of trouble. After many teeth-gritting years, they themselves may be promoted to director. They can then assume the same irritating mannerisms and habits.

Studio Engineers

Anyone who is in any way connected with the technical side of studio sound and vision is a manager or supervisor of some sort. So whereas the film sound man is called the Sound Recordist, the studio equivalent is the **Sound Supervisor**. Similarly the humble Sparks is transformed into a **Lighting Supervisor** or even **a Lighting Director**. To reflect the importance of their titles, these people also change their uniform. Production may think they're 'arty' in leather jackets and high-heels, film crews may be macho in their informality but studio engineers always wear ties. And no Lighting Manager or Sound Supervisor feels dressed without an ill-fitting jacket with obligatory screwdriver in the top pocket.

Outside Broadcasts

O.B.s are just like studios except that the gallery is in a van called a **scanner** and everyone else is outside or positioned around the theatre/concert hall/stadium track. The only extras are bacon-sandwich-touting location caterers and the piratical crew of O.B. **riggers**, a band whose tasks vary dramatically between the onerous job of setting up lights and stages and the less taxing job of hanging around the caterer's fragrant van or using spare moments (chargeable) for filling in overtime sheets.

Editing

Unless they are live, all programmes have to be edited or 'cut together'. Misleadingly, this is not done by the **Programme Editor** who is just a senior producer but by a **film** or **videotape editor**.

The rift between film craft and hi-tech studio engineering reaches its widest here. Film and tape editors are very different animals. Never confuse them: they get very angry.

First you must know that there is a fundamental difference in the materials with which they work. Film is a long strip of celluloid split into picture **frames**. So you can hold a bit up to the light and see what's on it. Videotape, however, is black stuff with pictures electronically recorded onto it. No amount of holding it up to the light or trying to shine torches through it will show what tape contains.

You must also know that film and tape are edited in very different ways. Film editors take the strips of film and accompanying sound-tape that make up **shots**, cut them up and stick the pieces together in order to make an edited **sequence**. But video editors record pictures from the **rushes** tape onto an **edited master** chunk by chunk. The whole process is electronic, no tape is ever physically cut.

As a result, the two breeds of editor scorn each other. Film editors delight in working in seedy basements with old bits of film hanging or flung about all over the place. Yet the film editor knows what and where everything is. Machinery is simple and spare and fixed with a screwdriver, a bit of wire or a kick. Film editors deride video editors for needing a king's ransom of transistors and chips plus three back-up and maintenance engineers before a single 'cut' can be made.

Video editors, on the other hand, are proud of their **suites** that look like the flight deck of Concorde. Fronted by a bank of monitors, they make edits by pressing lots of buttons and programming in long series of numbers called **timecodes**. They rarely, if ever, touch the actual videotape which is probably on machines half a mile away. Video editors ridicule film editors for being messy primitives using outdated materials and methods.

Finally, you should know a few technical terms in this area. Always refer to videotape as **VT** (BBC) or **VTR** (ITV) and film as **TK**. If a film looks good on screen say 'it must have been shot on **slow neg**. rather than **fast reversal**'. And be aware that editors, film or video, can only edit the material they have been given. So however much **post-production** there may be, a lousy idea lousily executed will inevitably end up as a lousy programme thanks to . . .

Production

The supposed creative side of programme making. **Producers** and **executive producers** have overall financial and artistic responsibility for programmes and series. Directors tell film crews and studios what to do. Some organisations get double value out of staff by employing individuals as 'producer-directors' or even 'producer-director-reporters'. The less producers and directors know, the more they talk and give orders.

Production Assistants (P.A.s) and secretaries deal with the administrative, clerical and budgeting sides of a programme. They know everything and prevent endless disasters. They are almost always women and thus generally underpaid and ignored.

PROGRAMMES

A detailed knowledge of programme contents is unnecessary. However you must know the available varieties of programme and the real reasons why they are made. Spice the mixture with a few classic titles and your guru status is assured.

News

News happens all the time. Or at least news programmes happen all the time – usually at fixed points in the schedule and with a fixed length. So whether there is a major international crisis or absolutely nothing of note to report, the same hole has to be filled, day in day out, with stories that are made to look as if they are important.

This need for importance rubs off on the television journalists. **Reporters** make themselves feel important by wearing trenchcoats (brought from their last local newspaper) – especially in summer. Senior reporters buttress their egos by becoming **correspondents** or even **special correspondents** and learning to speak in a deep voice. Even so they know nothing more about the subject. And almost anyone working behind the scenes calls themselves an 'editor'; this makes them feel immensely superior to the mere 'producers' in all other departments.

News people reinforce their position of supposed superiority by compounding jargon with abbreviations not even other television people can understand. Hence the title of a story becomes **the slug** while headlines become **the heads**. Unless, of course, you work on *News at Ten* in which case they're known universally as **the bongs**.

Everybody in news is obsessed by urgency. They're always rushing around the open-plan newsroom having **conferences** and **changing the running order** of stories. And scripts cannot possibly be written until the very last moment – even though the story itself is three days old. The panic doesn't stop during the programme either. Here the most senior editor of all the editors demonstrates authority by constantly juggling the bulletin around.

News supremos also devote much of their time to a never-ending revamp of the appearance of their programmes. The three favourites are:

a) new dramatic title sequences
b) new sets
c) new faces to read the scripts.

Occasionally bulletins are dramatized by putting the presenter in the middle of the newsroom with its litter of telephones, typewriters, fag ends, half-empty wine bottles and secretaries each being paid a 'staff contribution fee' for appearing 'in vision'. Look for the giveaway, the pile of newspapers from which the copy has been **researched** (i.e. stolen) in the first place.

But in spite of all the tinkering, The News (as distinct from the news) remains pretty much unchanged. Never forget that a story is really only a television news story if there happens to be a film crew present on the scene. No pictures, no story.

Current Affairs

These programmes tend to deal with the same sort of stories as news programmes, but they are designed to be longer and more tedious. This is to give the impression that the viewer who perseveres to the end will somehow have gained an in-depth understanding of the issues of the day. Sadly, length and substance bear little direct relationship.

The mainstay of any current affairs programme is the studio interview. If there is just one interviewee, it is referred to as a **one plus one**. If there are two interviewees, it is a **one plus two** and so on. Each interviewee is normally allocated three minutes of air time, since this is believed to be the precise length of time a viewer's attention is held. So you can see that it is a simple matter to fill programmes.

Because current affairs programmes are live, the main concern of any producer worth his or her salt is to ensure that the programme runs to exactly the right duration – preferably to the nearest second. This is why the presenter is usually equipped with a small plastic earpiece attached to a radio receiver. It's through this channel that the producer and director shout an unending stream of instructions and numbers designed to make every interview run exactly **to time**. The content of the interview is of secondary importance.

Bluffers should know that all presenters have their own personalised earpiece, fashioned from a mould made with hot wax poured in the ear. It's an unpleasant process but gives presenters a gruesome perspex-boxed status symbol to carry around.

It is worth knowing, too, that interviewees are selected not for their expertise but for the impressiveness of their **name super** – the on-screen credit flashed up when an interviewee appears. Thus for an item on animal welfare, Dr. Zebediah von Turtlecuddler from the Worldwide Homoeopathic Snake Nursing Foundation will always be preferred to top vet Pete Brown.

You should remember that all contemporary current affairs programmes are mediocre. They are only thought of as brilliant long after they have been taken off the air. Thus you can eulogise about the journalistic strengths of the BBC's *Tonight* programme in the 1960s ('it established the concept of personality reporters') or, from the same stable, *That Was the Week That Was* ('an ingenious fusion of topicality and biting humour'). More recently, *Nationwide* was identified as an important milestone in factual television with its revolutionary technique of '**hot-switch up-country linking**' which led to the much-parodied 'regional round-up'. It is also permissible to praise foreign programmes – the American *Sixty Minutes* programme is regularly referred to in glowing terms by broadcasting executives who have never seen it.

Finally, remember that current affairs programmes are very inexpensive to make. In fact they represent the cheapest form of television yet invented, second only to . . .

Sport

All you need to make a sports programme is an outside broadcast van, equipped with four or five cameras. Set up the cameras in strategic positions round a playing field/tennis court/dart board/mousehole and you're in business. Once the power is switched on an endless stream of ready 'entertainment' is available for virtually no additional cost. Even the performers usually don't have to be paid – they rely on large handouts from sponsoring companies to make their appearance worthwhile. The sponsoring companies in turn rely on spattering their name all over the screen to make their investment worthwhile. And they succeed with flying colours.

This enables the bluffer to put television sport in a new light. Explain caustically that the soft drink consumed between sets at Wimbledon has more to do with a thirst for money than anything else. Similarly football trophies are held at a height that best displays the brand name on a winning captain's shirt. And racing drivers only crash by a sponsor's hoarding.

Thus all sports programmes are commercial television, however hard the BBC may deny it.

Drama

The first play ever broadcast on television was Pirandello's *The Man with the Flower in his Mouth* made in London for Logie Baird in 1930. It featured a man and a flower but not much else and few people saw it.

The same has been true for most serious drama programmes ever since. Although they may be the product of months or years of meticulous preparation, they rarely attract a large audience. This is not to say that they are worthless; in fact as a general rule, audience size and critical acclaim are inversely related. Drama on television is also immensely expensive.

Whether or not you've seen any television drama doesn't matter. No one else will have done so either. But it is a subject on which you can hold forth with great authority. Drama is divided into:

a) single plays
b) serials
c) series.

There is no good reason for this but television people like it that way.

Always talk about **single plays** not in terms of their plot, acting or quality of production but in terms of their Importance. Thus *Cathy Come Home*, shown in the 1960s, was a good play because its social statement was Important. *The War Game*, made at about the same time but not shown until some twenty years later, was on the same grounds even more Important. And *Scum* is Very Important. So Important that it will probably never get transmitted.

Drama serials, on the other hand, can be praised for more mundane reasons – beautiful costumes, exotic locations or (a good one to throw in) 'the accuracy of the characterisation'. Included in the hall of fame for this type of drama are *The Forsyte Saga*, *Brideshead Revisited* and *The Jewel in the Crown*. Provided a drama serial is at least ten programmes long, you can always assume that there will be a hospital scene, a society wedding and at least one shooting. Mention these as memorable high points (or low points) and no one will argue; the vast majority of viewers never get beyond the second episode.

Drama series are a set of self-contained episodes yet every week featuring the same characters. Many would say they also feature the same plot. With drama series it's either cult or bust. You should know about both successes and failures. In the case of successes know the title and catch-phrase. Classics are *Dixon of Dock Green* ('Evening all'), *Minder* (' 'Er indoors'/'Nice little earner') and *Doctor Who* ('Exterminate! Exterminate!'). In the cases of failures, invent your own titles and characters. Few things are as forgotten as a failed drama series and your fund of obscure 'knowledge' will only add to your status.

To speak with authority about drama you really need two more things:

1. Strong opinions about the **score** (i.e. the music) and the **motivation** (reason why) underlying any bit of drama.
2. A deep reverence for some obscure name picked at random from the credits.

Because drama producers became frustrated with making programmes where the cast outnumbers the viewers, they invented . . .

Soaps

Soap operas, or 'contemporary drama series' as their makers call them, are the runaway ratings success of television. They get their name from the pioneering days of American commercial broadcasting, when early examples of the genre were often sponsored by washing-powder manufacturers.

These days it doesn't matter where you live, you're bound to be surrounded by soap-watchers, soap-makers and soap-actors. In Britain more than a third of the population watches one or more soaps every day. In America a twiddle of the dial brings you a round-the-clock soap service. And in China the top soap is the world's most popular programme: *Four Generations Under One Roof* which pulls in an audience of nearly 500 million for every enigmatic oriental episode.

Nowadays there are almost as many soap-lives being lived as real ones. And it's often hard for devotees to tell the difference. If in doubt, they assume the soap is true and that their own lives are just an unfortunate error in a rejected script.

For the bluffer, soaps are straightforward. Made by sausage-machine production, every soap has a rolling plot that consists entirely of middle, never beginning or end. Thus familiarity with the minutiae of a particular ratings-buster and its colourful characters is unnecessary. All soaps contain the same ingredients, so once you know the recipe, you can cook up an authoritative opinion or armchair analysis with ease.

Recognise the simple formula: start with a location, people it with the expected stereotypes, put them in the situations dictated by their setting, profession and social class and watch them 'inter-react'.

Traditionally it was a hospital with caring good-looking male doctors, strict matrons and swooning nurses (*Dr Kildare*, *Emergency Ward Ten*) or American Everywheresville and small-town morality (*Peyton Place*). Then came the turn of the chummy working class and problems that were naughty but nice (*Coronation Street* – always referred to as just '*The Street*'). But American producer **Aaron Spelling**, realising that the rich could afford to indulge in more juicy forms of angst, invented *Dallas* and *Dynasty*, where death, adultery, alcohol and deceit were carefully blended with haute couture, white Rolls and lip-gloss.

All this, you must point out, is old stetson. Nowadays the key phrase is 'social realism'. All human life is here: no baby can be born unless it's illegitimate; no cigarette contains anything but drugs; no money (and ideally there should be no money) can change hands unless it's stolen. But despite abject misery, hardship and deprivation, everyone stays remarkably chummy.

And social realism is very expensive. In *Eastenders* jolly cockneys do the business in a replica of a real East End square, built in Hertfordshire at a cost of a million pounds. No wonder the less affluent TV networks of Australia are sticking through thick and thin to the cardboard cheapness of the tried and tested: *The Young Doctors* still heart-throb the nurses there.

Finally, note that however like ordinary people soap characters may seem, they never do the one thing that real people do most – watching TV. Especially not themselves.

Light Entertainment

There are two types of light entertainment (always abbreviated by practitioners to **light ent.** or just **L.E.**) – comedy and variety.

Comedy

Comedy, as its name implies, is meant to be funny. It rarely is. Even so there have been some notable exceptions.

From the early days, you have to like *Hancock* although you should point out that the radio version was infinitely better. The same scriptwriters, **Galton** and **Simpson**, created 'social realism' **sitcom** (situation comedy) in the sixties with *Steptoe and Son*; a form that was pushed to its useful limits by **Johnny Speight**'s wall-to-wall insults with **Alf Garnett** in *Til Death Us Do Part* (catchphrase: 'Shut up, you silly old moo.') which the Americans copied when creating *All in the Family*.

Be careful when you mention *Monty Python's Flying Circus*: there are still a lot of Python Bores at large – people who can recite in full the famous 'Parrot' and 'Cheese Shop' sketches verbatim and even backwards.

Other comedy milestones include the American import, *Rowan and Martin's Laugh-In* ('The concept of the catchphrase explored to its utmost'), *Fawlty Towers* – notably the episode with the Germans – and *The Young Ones* ('A brilliant vehicle for packaging the previously minority-orientated alternative humour into a mass audience format').

Remember that for the bluffer the essential interest of these programmes is not their amusement value. Construction is what counts. For example, the average sitcom is allowed a maximum of three sets and rarely has more than half a dozen characters. If there are more, they are entirely two-dimensional and can be replaced or sacrificed without anybody noticing. The script too conforms to a set pattern. Watch out for the **running gag** (the same joke becoming supposedly funnier by endless repetition), the crudely predictable **set-up** and **punch** lines and the improbable **sinker** – an early irrelevance that miraculously and contortedly ties up in time for the credits.

Comedy is also a useful vehicle for pronouncements on national character. What makes a nation laugh can be taken to illustrate its preoccupations. In America, for example, comedy is varied, slickly and quickly made but blandly manufactured. What makes the Brazilians and the Germans laugh is slapstick and even more than usually ludicrous excesses of passion. For the Japanese, the best jokes are based around someone getting something sharp up the backside. In the Low Countries and Scandinavia nothing is considered very funny.

Variety

The other branch of light entertainment, variety, is standardised all over the world. The inevitable ingredients are a studio, an audience and a quota of

personalities. Most of these 'personalities' are ageing pop singers who have long outlived their last hit record and have failed to do the decent thing by dying dramatically at an early age. The normal format includes about six songs (mimed to a pre-recorded backing track), a couple of dance routines (with the emphasis on routine) and a celebrity guest appearance, the celebrity being another 'personality' who is doing the rounds. Applause and laughter account for some 15 per cent of the programme content; since neither programme nor audience are up to this standard, canned effects are dubbed on afterwards.

Variety programmes should always be rubbished. Nowadays, thankfully, these programmes are on the decline. This is largely because of the ascendancy in their place of . . .

Chat Shows

Originally a humble interviewer in obsequious conversation with a star, chat shows are now vehicles for the star interviewer with the guest coming a poor second. Thus such inventive programme titles as *Parkinson*, *Harty* and *Wogan*.

You should know that all chat show hosts are vastly overpaid and do very little work. Their scripts, briefs and questions are written by the researchers who also find and book the guests. You should know too that most chat show hosts are tubby and disguise it by sitting in special chairs. Their favourite part of the programme is the opening monologue which they extend interminably while the guests are kept waiting just off stage in a small and uncomfortable booth known as the 'tremble box'.

Guests come in three varieties:

1. The person who has something to sell or plug, usually a book, a record or another programme on the same network. These will always express well rehearsed surprise when asked the pre-arranged questions about their product.
2. The chat show old-timer. These 'celebrities' are tried and tested 'good talkers' guaranteed to maunder on pleasantly and to order. They are kept up the sleeve of every chat show producer for use when no-one else can be found.
3. A much smaller category: real people with a genuine and topical story to charm the heart of the nation. Although good for ratings appeal, they are hated by host and producer alike for their inability to deliver an anecdote on cue or hit a punch line in time for the commercial break.

Much easier to tame and humiliate are the suckers on:

Game Shows

For the bluffer there's no gamble at all in game shows. They are a fecund source of curiosities, comment and behind-the-scenes anecdote. Of course, for the actual contestants it's not like that at all. They are the squeaking white mice in a laboratory-honed piece of mass entertainment. And the person who rattles their cages with consummate skill is the real star of the show: **the host**.

Game shows have matured considerably over the years. The Americans realised early on that what was needed was a controlled, reliable format where semi-hysterical contestants would just 'be themselves' or display a little low animal cunning. You can cite with approval the incredible longevity of *Let's Make a Deal* or the skilful schmaltz of *Queen For a Day* (where the woman with the most appalling hard-luck story was palliated by being crowned). Since then America has progressed steadily, producing ever more sophisticated pieces of audience and contestant manipulation. Point out that prospective contestants will actually train to get on *The Dating Game* (much more humiliating than the watered-down British copy, *Blind Date*) or the Manhattan cable show where men and women gradually and publicly strip each other naked.

In general British game shows are cosier. The British even enjoy the antiquated format of the wireless legacy of quizzes. In programmes like *Call My Bluff* and *Face the Music* contestants are professional and real competition and the humiliation of defeat are gone. Hold a strong view on these quizzes. Either they are rigged and chintzy or they show a warming degree of sanity. Contrast them with the Japanese *Ultra Quiz* where contestants are taken all over the world to endure physical agony and psychological injury for the sake of one large prize and avoiding the dreaded Eastern loss of face.

Bear in mind that almost all new game shows are reworks of old game shows, but made simpler. The questions require only a 'yes' or 'no' answer and are rarely difficult. Thus nobody can do too well and even a moron will perform respectably. Atmosphere and tension are generated by basing the show around catchphrases orchestrated by the compere and by encouraging audience participation.

The most successful game shows have all these elements. Thus Bruce Forsyth's *Play Your Cards Right* is brilliantly whipped along by frenzied shouts of 'Higher, Higher' and 'Lower, Lower'. And *The Price Is Right* is the quintessence with its wealth of audience 'advice', its catchphrase 'Come on Down' and its suggestion that everybody knows the value of money.

Be cynical about modern game shows: they are a cunningly cheap operation. They are made even cheaper by being recorded in batches. When the compere and contestants wave goodbye as the credits roll, the day is far from over in the studio. On the quiz shows like *Call My Bluff* there's a short break while the professional contestants change suits and dresses before recording 'next week's edition'. But real game shows go straight on. In America three shows is a standard recording, and the teenage game show *Blockbusters* records up to eight at one sitting. It's a bargain for the TV companies, but studio audiences at some shows have to be locked in.

The final factor that keeps quiz shows cheap is the rules regarding the value of prizes. This alters from country to country. In America it is still possible to win a million dollars, but in Nigeria the top prize in the highest rating game show is a transistor radio. The second prize is regularly a packet of soap powder. In Britain the situation is somewhere in between. For commercial television the IBA has ruled that there must be an average value of not more than £8,000 worth of prizes won per show. So if the family car has been won two weeks running, it's unlikely there'll be such a big prize available the third week. The BBC limit is very much lower. If the car has been won on a BBC game show for the last two weeks, this week's contestants should seriously consider whether they wouldn't win bigger prizes in Nigeria.

At the opposite pole of human experience from game shows comes . . .

Religion

There are countries where it's hard to tell where game shows stop and religion begins. America with its constitutional right to freedom of religious expression has a host of TV evangelists armed with rock bands, donation lines and good ole down-home rhetoric. All are asking the same question: will your soul be saved?

But the blatantness of the American message is unique. In most places the problems of Religious Programmes are rather different. The concern these days is with subtlety. This means pretending that what is being presented isn't really Religion at all.

The main move here has been to try and fool the audience by taking Religion out of what is known in the business as **the God Slot** – early evening on Sundays – and put it on at funny times of the day or week. So by the time you realise you're watching a religious programme it's too late.

Science

Science programmes are very popular not least because the scientific content is diluted to an absolute minimum. Unlike news or current affairs broadcasts, presenters of science programmes should never look or behave like normal human beings: instead squeaking kindergarten enthusiasm or, better still, mannerism and eccentricity are the order of the day. Thus in Britain the miracles of science have turned into household names the unlikely figures of **Patrick Moore** (who averages 240 words per minute), **Magnus Pyke** (a retired civil servant who waves his arms about frantically) and **David Bellamy** (a bearded botanist with a speech defect).

There is no logic about which branches of science make 'good television'. Medicine is invariably popular – especially if colourful operating table sequences are included. But undoubtedly your prime concern must be with TV science's greatest hit: natural history programmes. Essentially, the prestige of any natural history series is directly proportional to the distance travelled to film it. Thus the feeding habits of barn owls in Hertfordshire are of minimal interest; film the same breed of owls in the rain forests of Mexico and you've obtained 'a unique insight into the frontiers of man's understanding of his environment'. Similarly no two consecutive sequences must be filmed on the same continent; the only feature they should have in common is **David Attenborough**.

Finally point out that although natural history programmes look glossy and expensive, they aren't: animals are like game show contestants – they don't get paid.

Children's Programmes

There are only two children's programmes, past or present, with which you ever need to concern yourself. The first is, was and always will be *Blue Peter*.

It's been going for more than a generation and although its presenters may come and go the formula stays delightfully the same: 'nice and firmly' was its catch phrase and 'nice and firmly' has always been the attitude to its viewers.

You should know that the original presenters were **Valerie Singleton** and **Christopher Trace** but they soon became a trio with the addition of **John** 'get down, Shep' **Noakes**. Be aware too that this pattern

38

of two men and a woman may well be a piece of cunning child psychology, based on the stereotypes of 'dependable dad', 'good old mum' and 'me daft big brother'.

But as well as being safely dependable, *Blue Peter* is also slightly unpredictable; its live transmission lures viewers with the promise of another classic studio disaster. Everybody knows about the famous defecating pachyderm; cap it with the Brownies campfire conflagration and the pets that ate each other.

Finally point out that however matey it all looks, *Blue Peter* is far from blue – the presenters are not even allowed to touch.

The other milestone of children's television is *Watch with Mother*. Its golden era was the 1960's and the constant repetition of its limited stock of programmes ensured their status in popular culture. You must know the big three and their consequences: *Andy Pandy* created a fashion for the one-piece, candy-striped boiler suit; *The Flowerpot Men* (catchphrase: 'Flob-ob-dee-ob-weeb') inspired a disturbingly druggy pop group; *The Woodentops* set the style for silly walks and a million dogs called 'Spotty'.

Children's programmes have always been designed to appeal to both young viewers and, more importantly, their parents. Unfortunately there is a rebellious block in between, known uncomfortably as 'teenagers' or, worse, 'young adults'. It was in pursuit of this audience that middle-aged TV producers in leather jackets created the excruciating failure known as:

Youth Programmes

Start with a screen test: look for anyone who has reasonable performing skills, personality and intelligence. Send them away. Keep the biggest nobody that remains – if he or she has acne, so much the better. 'Street cred' for this audience definitely includes pimples.

The underlying philosophy or 'big thing' about youth programmes is that everyone's life is constantly beset by terrible problems – medical, sexual, quasi-sexual, and car problems. These are attacked with earnest discussion sugared every three minutes by 'fun' in the shape of unfunny studio events and pop music performed by unknowns.

There are no classic youth programmes.

Documentaries

A documentary is produced by taking a camera away from its normal television environment and letting it run in the unlikely hope that the lives and sayings of **real people** will render special insights and the incontrovertible wisdom of the university of life.

Documentaries can therefore be made about anything. In the early days this made life easy for would-be film makers and earnest young television producers fresh from Oxford or Cambridge. Little had yet been seen on television so all you had to do to make a passable documentary was: be there first. If the situation was dirty or unpleasant, you scored extra points.

Now, many thousands of documentaries later, it's all changed. Everyone has already seen the definitive sufferings of oppressed tin-miners in Latvia, and all the caustic corners of *Whickers World*. So it's a lot more difficult to find anything new to make.

Two solutions have been found:

1. Get a million pounds from a foreign co-producer and make a mega-series on a Big Subject: *Civilisation*, *Life on Earth*, *Cosmos*.
2. Make more and more about less and less. Here highly specialized subjects are chosen: Channel 4 has transmitted an hour-long international documentary on the human foot.

Arts Programmes

To many people arts programmes sprang fully fledged from the mind of **Huw Wheldon** (*q.v.*) editor and figurehead of *Monitor*, the classic BBC arts documentary series of the early 1960s. He was a charming and adventurous man, which makes him unusual in television. On *Monitor* he helped and encouraged talented young directors. This again was policy diametrically opposed to that of most contemporaries and successors.

The result was some classic films still regularly plundered by impoverished modern producers. The film that every bluffer must know is **Ken Russell**'s *Elgar*. Here for the first time an actor was used to represent the composer though the film was documentary rather than drama. It was shot mute and given a sound track of music and Huw Wheldon's commentary. You can get extra credibility by knowing that commentary for the entire programme was recorded in a single take and contains two or three stumbles. You should also know that of Russell's other music films for *Monitor*, *Richard Strauss* was destroyed after a single showing because of opposition from the composer's family.

The only classic programmes you really need

41

acknowledge are *The South Bank Show, Omnibus* and *Arena. The South Bank Show* referred to simply as *S.B.S.*, is presented by Melvyn. *Omnibus* deals with people who are 'major' and 'International' and likes to avoid having a presenter. *Arena* aims to be mould-breaking, contemporary and not afraid to deal with the icons of popular culture. It likes to employ people with several days' growth of stubble.

Education

The sad truth about most TV education programmes is that hardly anyone watches them; the size of the production team regularly exceeds that of the audience.

Schools programmes do get at least some audience simply because their viewers are forced to watch.

Adult education programmes (referred to in the industry as **Continuing Education** or just **C.E.**) also get audiences that are 'ratings perceptible'. This is because they are made to be so short (5 or 10 minutes) that people don't bother to switch off after the preceding programme.

The Open University offers a wealth of opportunities for the bluffer. The inaccessibility of its programmes makes anyone who watches them not only an intellectual but someone of considerable stamina. Whether or not you do actually see any of these programmes is irrelevant; you can express a strong opinion about any or all of them in the absolutely certain knowledge that in the course of a human lifetime you will never meet anyone else who could know any better.

GREAT NAMES

There are many people in television's short history who would like to be considered its pioneers. Few people can remember who they are. Broadly speaking these also-rans fall into three categories.

1. The performers who think they are intellectuals: current affairs presenters in particular suffer from this as does everybody else who has to work with them.
2. The intellectuals who also fancy themselves as performers.
3. The small group who present themselves as both performers and intellectuals but aren't either.

The really great names of television can be counted on the fingers of both hands – at most you may have to take off a sock. The bluffer need only be familiar with the following list, blue-chip characters whose names may safely be mentioned both inside and outside the business.

Lord Reith

Although 'Reith' did not have much to do with television, you need to know about him because he invented the BBC. From humble beginnings in a shed at Writtle in Essex he saw his business grow to occupy the formidable Broadcasting House in central London, a building which for no apparent reason was designed by a naval architect and so looks like a battleship. Today it is said that his ghost still haunts the management suite on the third floor.

Reith's legacy is 'Reithian values' – a vague code of moral probity and commitment to the purity of Public Service Broadcasting. Reith himself was actually an extremely foul-mouthed man with enormous feet, and what he really thought is largely forgotten.

Hugh Greene

Full name Sir Hugh Carleton Greene, he is not to be confused with Hughie *Opportunity Knocks* Green or the Clap-o-meter. Like Reith, Hugh Greene became Director General of the BBC some 40 years later on.

With a name like Carleton Greene, it seemed to the Governors who appointed him that he would be a safe conservative option for the job. In fact he was disturbingly radical and supported makers of innovative and risqué programmes. The governors were wary of making such a mistake again.

Lew Grade

One of the first moguls of commercial television, Grade lived for work. He had three telephones in every room of his penthouse, including the sauna, and he arrived for work at 6.30 a.m. But he is chiefly legendary for founding a television dynasty and for his endless consumption of elephantine cigars. Unfortunately, he is also ultimately responsible for *Crossroads*.

Grace Wyndham Goldie

Although her position as head of current affairs at the BBC was never one of the topmost top jobs, she is broadcasting's token female management success. Thus she has become the idol for chauvinist male executives, the cocks of the industry's walk.

Even today, years after she retired, you can still hear sighs of relief coming from BBC management suites. With Grace Wyndham Goldie as ammunition, no woman need be allowed up to their level again.

Sir Huw Wheldon

Wheldon's initial foray into television showed little promise of his future greatness: he presented the children's programme *All Your Own*. Here the only remarkable event was that a competition to find Britain's biggest conker attracted a postbag of 58,000 globular lumps of vegetable matter.

Wheldon really began to make his name when he devised, edited and presented *Monitor* (*q.v.*). As the BBC's Managing Director of Television ('M.D.Tel'), he was creative, witty and memorably outspoken. Once he listed no fewer than 29 reasons for disliking a particular documentary, his remarks sprinkled with four-letter words in the best Reithian traditions.

David Frost

It is for the ease with which he entered the industry in the first place that Frost is most admired and envied. After a disastrous six-month contract with the ITV Rediffusion company, where he presented a single programme called *Let's Twist on the Riviera . . .*, he stepped straight into the BBC – not as a lowly trainee, but as presenter of the innovative and satirical *That Was The Week That Was*.

In 1967 he put together a successful consortium for the coveted London Weekend Television franchise. He himself presented three prime time programmes: *Frost on Friday*, *Frost on Saturday* and the distinctively different *Frost on Sunday*. The audience responded en masse by switching over to the BBC.

Fifteen years later, as a founder member of the TV-am Breakfast Station, he introduced an item about disabled people with 'And now from nuclear arms let's turn to people with no arms'. Once again the audiences switched over to the BBC.

The 'Tonight' Reporters
In the early 1960s *Tonight* (*q.v.*) created personality
reporters: not just a voice but a face, the odd
mannerism and even an unusual jacket. These 'characters' were all men. Women were not allowed to become
personalities until years later.

You should point out that this bunch of heroes (**Fyfe
Robertson, Alan Whicker** and other forgotten
names) was not exactly carefully selected: the BBC
just got lucky. They were bought in as a job lot from
the recently defunct *Picture Post*.

Richard Dimbleby
Dimbleby was the original heavyweight broadcaster.
He became the first BBC wireless reporter, his position
helped by being allowed to draw up his job description
himself. For years he filed stories from far-flung war
zones, recording his despatches on small shellac discs
which had to be smuggled back to England to be broadcast. Eventually he escaped from the trenches and took
on the equally perilous role of presenter of the first
televised General Election programme.

Your view of Richard Dimbleby should be one of
nostalgic reverence: the millions spent on computer
graphics in today's election programmes are clearly no
substitute for Dimbleby's informed authority.

Dimbleby was also the original front-man for the
BBC's *Panorama* programme, in BBC-speak the
'flagship' of Current Affairs. It is an odd reflection of
television's attitude to journalism that, on his death,
the signature tune was changed as a mark of respect
from the allegro of a Rachmaninov symphony to the
incidental music from *Un Homme et Une Femme*, a
low-budget, French love matinée.

Sir Robin Day

Originally a barrister, he was one of the first news-readers at ITN, where he shared the presenting with Jeremy Thorpe. He then moved to the BBC where he has remained ever since. Bluffers should highlight his acerbic style and the fact that this led an enraged Tory minister, John Nott, to storm out of a live interview.

Reginald Bosanquet

As with Sir Robin, 'Reggie' Bosanquet first rose to national prominence as an ITN newsreader. But instead of leaving the job, he stuck at it and developed it into a highly personal artform; throughout the 1970s he was to all intents and purposes *the* television newsreader.

His popularity relied on the combination of a lop-sided smile, an obvious toupé and slurred delivery – he always claimed that this was absolutely nothing to do with his fondness for drink, it was instead caused by a 'faulty facial muscle'. He frequently went on air with a broomstick stuffed up the back of his jacket to ensure that his 'muscle problem' did not cause him to keel over. Audiences rose as the odds that he might not make it to the end of a bulletin grew ever shorter. Of course he always did; he was a television professional to the very last gulp.

Walter Cronkite

Although Reggie transformed newsreading from Autocue into unsteady art, he never matched the global celebrity or concerned gravitas of America's 'Uncle Walter'. For twenty years Cronkite presented the nightly CBS news, blending fact with his own distinctive style of opinionated analysis.

Cronkite's strong following among the middle-class, middle-American heartland led Lyndon Johnson to concede that being President was only the second most powerful job in the U.S.A.

Like many other famed broadcasters, Cronkite's gimmick was his catch-phrase: all America imitated his inevitable signing-off line, 'And that's the way it is'. No rival network could find a newsreader as loved or believed as Walter Cronkite. Even when he retired in 1981, CBS had the business sense to keep Cronkite on their books as a 'special correspondent' for the modest retainer of a million dollars a year.

Johnny Carson

The king of chat shows and the only other American broadcaster you need know. His *Tonight* programme (always introduced by the off-screen announcement 'Heeeeeere's Johnny!') has never been rivalled.

Because he is far more important than nearly all the 'celebrities' who appear on his show, he has no compunction about being rude to them. Easily bored, he frequently starts whistling or tapping his pencil in the middle of an interview. He also has a permanent sidekick, Ed McMahon, who has become a household name in his own right solely by wearing dreadful checked jackets and laughing unctuously at Carson's jokes.

The only other thing you need to know about Johnny Carson is that he is very, very, very rich. When his third wife divorced him in 1985, she collected $3.5 million in cash as well as four homes, three cars and a Picasso. This left him with just five homes, three cars and the lucrative rights to video recordings of twenty years of his own programme.

Appearing on Television

Sooner or later everyone appears on television. Even if you live in a mud hut in Borneo, some enterprising producer (on expenses) is bound to arrive with a film crew (on double expenses) and demand an interview. It's worth knowing a few tips to ensure your fleeting moment of media stardom is a success.

The **vox pop** is supposed to be a brief pull together of public opinion on some topical news story. In this case the 'public' is usually unwary shoppers caught in the precinct nearest the studios. A **shooting ratio** of 10 to 1 is customary – i.e. only one tenth of the film shot will be used. To make sure your contribution makes it on to the air, remember the following rules:

a) Speak in short self-contained sentences with gaps in between (easy to edit out a nice short chunk).

b) Express a strong view (whether or not it reflects your true opinion). Phrases like 'public scandal', 'he'll have to resign' or 'bring back the noose' are useful here.

c) Try to make it funny. If you cannot think of anything amusing to say, adopt a silly voice or mannerism – definitely **good television**.

A more challenging encounter with television cameras is the studio interview. Politicians know the importance of getting it right which is why they spend thousands of pounds going to special television training schools run by failed producers.

Your audition is a telephone call from a programme researcher trying to find out whether or not you are a **good talker**. Only if you speak fluently and express a strong view (again, your true opinion is irrelevant) will you be chosen.

If you pass, you must consider your personal appearance. Wear the right clothes. Avoid anything with a check or criss-cross pattern; this causes **strobing**, an interference with the coloured lines on a television picture that appears as a swirling psychedelic mess. Anyone with strobing clothes is a laughing stock.

It's also important to sit correctly. The presenter will almost certainly be sitting on a slightly higher chair to create an impression of dominance and authority over programme guests. When being interviewed, sit up straight to reduce the imbalance.

You should establish how long the interview will last and then make a list of the three or four positive points you intend to make. The questions themselves do not matter – they must be disposed of quickly and effectively to clear the way for what you really want to say. A typical device is to pretend you've already answered the question, even if you haven't. Another old favourite is to get the viewers on your side by suggesting the presenter's choice of subjects is misguidedly esoteric, e.g.

PRESENTER: Why has the inflation rate trebled in just one month?

INTERVIEWEE: I've already made that clear. And, frankly, that's not the issue that's uppermost in people's minds at the moment. The key concern now is the very real problem of income tax. And that's why we've reduced taxes by more than any government in the last three hundred years.

Finally, always remember to look the presenter straight in the eye – this makes you look sincere. And NEVER lose your temper: the typical viewer is female, fifty-five and living in a suburban estate. Research shows that the typical viewer thinks people who shout are 'not very nice'.

AFTER THE PROGRAMME

For the viewer, a television programme ends when the last credit fades to black. For the television professional, the programme is only the start – just the first stage in a lengthy process of analysis, criticism and introspection which provides the real creative challenge.

The Ratings Game

Every television producer will profess loudly and assertively that ratings are irrelevant: 'quality, innovation and critical acclaim are all that matters'. This is, of course, a lie. In practice, everyone in broadcasting, whether commercial or public service, is obsessed with viewing figures.

In Britain the weekly TV ratings are compiled by **B.A.R.B**. (The Broadcast Audience Research Bureau). These are available to senior television producers on a special hotline every Friday morning. Only fools ask any favours of their bosses before the smoke has cleared from last week's viewing figures.

You should know that ratings are compiled by two separate methods, the one intended as a cross-check on the other. Unfortunately both systems are methodologically flawed.

The first measure of audience numbers (which you should always refer to simply as the **T.V.R.**, Television Viewing Ratio) is derived from the records of the 'black boxes' attached to 2,000 television sets in a 'representative cross-section of British homes'. Your position must be one of scathing ridicule that something taken as seriously as the T.V.R. should rely in part on such a crude low-tech system.

The black box only records whether the set is switched on and which channel is selected. But how many people are actually watching is quite a different matter. In 1985 a study was conducted by Oxford University in which cameras were hidden inside domestic television sets to watch watchers watching. It found that most 'viewers' use the television simply as moving wallpaper, vying for attention with the fish tank or one of those lamps with lumps of wax floating about inside. Generally people also do something else: read a book, feed the cat, make love or just stare at the little black box on top of the television.

The second method of ratings measurement – 'the sample' – sounds clinical but is equally fallacious. Here some 3,000 people are stopped in the street every day and asked to recount in detail what they watched the night before. Most can't remember. So they are prompted instead with **Retrospective Viewing Choices**, such as: 'Did you watch *Wittgenstein: Profile of a Thinking Man* or the *Wham-Bam-It's - Your - Big - Money - Super - Prize - Knockabout - Jubilee-Show* on the other channel?' Invariably the respondents refuse to admit their true tastes and lie in favour of the most intellectual option presented. Alternatively there is the Inverted Snob Syndrome, a blanket refusal ever to watch anything on BBC 2 or Channel 4.

If at the end of this shaky process a producer finds that his T.V.R. is low, all is not yet lost. Hope is pinned instead on the **Appreciation Index** or **A.I.** as it is known. This purports to be a measure not of how many people were watching but how much the audience liked the programme. The A.I. is measured on a scale of 1–100; 80 or above is good, 60–80 is reasonable, 40–60 is disappointing; below 40 and either the producer is fired or the station proudly claims that 'the programme was ahead of its time'. Or both.

Awards

Although people working in television will never admit it, most programmes are instantly and totally forgettable. So to perpetuate faltering memories of transient images, more and more people in broadcasting look to an ever-growing number of awards as the only tangible result of an otherwise insubstantial product. For BBC producers in particular, an award in the hand is worth two years in Shepherd's Bush.

Award ceremonies are always too long and hopelessly self-congratulatory. Watch out for the 'award establishment', a motley collection of industry veterans who have long since outlived their useful programme-making life. They no longer qualify for any award based on actual production, but this is rarely a problem. Instead they invent other categories 'to recognise outstanding achievements in a lifetime of dedicated service' and take it in turn to award them to each other.

Nowadays, television award ceremonies are designed to be television programmes in their own right. This should only increase your scepticism: the very televising of the event distorts the event itself. To begin with the short-list of nominees is always heavily biased in favour of those who are prepared to come to the ceremony in person: seeing the award collected by the assistant director's assistant's best friend is definitely bad television. It also shows the world that no one cares about this award anyway.

You can further reveal that when short clips of nominated programmes are shown before the final verdict is announced, they are carefully selected to include only mediocre extracts from the runners-up and the very best bit of the winner. This is done to reinforce viewer perception of fair play and the wisdom of the judges; with a bit of practice you can rely on this principle to become an infallible armchair jurist well before the victory envelope is ceremonially opened.

Finally don't be too impressed by great demonstrations of ersatz impromptu emotion, and seemingly brilliant off-the-cuff acceptance speeches. The viewers are the only ones who don't know the results well in advance: winners and losers have been told beforehand to minimize embarrassing outbursts and ensure the programme runs neatly to time.

TV Tech

The BBC Globe
'Of course, you know, it doesn't exist' is the line here. The globe used to be an actual rotating model but is now just a silicon chip cheat. Point out that the very existence of the globe illustrates the Corporation's obsession with keeping a Respectful Distance. With the BBC you get the globe and a disembodied voice speaking King's English while on ITV you see a friendly continuity announcer with a regional accent and a comfy chair.

Cue Dots
Look in the top corner of the screen. With thirty seconds to go to the end of a programme you will usually see a couple of small white marks appear. At ten seconds to the end of the programme they vanish.

These cue dots serve to warn the next programme or continuity announcer that their hour is at hand. Don't tell anyone else about them. Just show a mysterious ability to count a programme out of existence.

Electronic Effects

These cause pictures to spin, twirl, turn like pages or disappear up the presenter's nose. The key word to mouth here is 'Quantel' – the name of the machine that does most of these effects. Don't try to explain how it works; just say that it's never been used properly. Say that its abuse is all part of what Peter Jay called 'the bias against understanding'.

Interview Trickery

1. When a presenter in a studio does a live interview with someone who is elsewhere (a **down-the-line** interview), the person being questioned generally appears in front of the presenter on a screen in the studio. This is your opportunity. Tell your fellow viewers that this is Chromakey or Colour Separation Overlay, and that the presenter isn't looking at the interviewee at all but staring at a blue or green box painted on the wall. The picture of the person being questioned is electronically placed in this coloured area only when the picture is transmitted. Although the viewer sees it, the presenter doesn't.

2. A film crew only carries one camera. In a filmed interview it is pointed at the person being questioned. If the reporter is ever shown asking the questions these have to be filmed separately. Such **reverse questions** are filmed after the interview is over sometimes on a different day, frequently in another place. So is the **noddy**, the technical term for a reporter's silent head-shaking reaction to what is being said by an inter-

viewee. It's used when editing the final film to cover the join when two completely unrelated sections of speech are spliced together to make one continuous statement. Thus a reporter's smile, frown or look of heavy concern are emotional reactions to nothing.

Global Vision

For the real bluffer the narrow limits of nationalism should never be enough. Your knowledge and interest in the medium must take account of the spreading electronic umbrella of international television and its effect on world culture. In other words, know a few recherché facts about how other people do it and you can get yourself instant admiration.

These days everyone has television. Even the eskimoes have it: mention that their main channel up at the North Pole is called Inuit TV and no-one but a polar bear will argue. The only nation which has been significantly unimpressed by television is India which still prefers the ancient wireless and the cinema.

In general there are two philosophies of programming. Some countries are obsessed with the need for television to be 'socially and artistically responsible'. Others rejoice in constant, schmaltzy entertainment with no pretence to anything more serious.

Britain is in the first category. Dogged by the ghost of Reith (*q.v.*), companies ride on a constant guilt cycle. The pressure to get high ratings generates the supremacy of populist tat. This is followed by the inevitable British backlash, with critics and the public bemoaning the 'disgusting fall in standards'. The television management is reshuffled, a new batch of 'serious and meaningful' programmes is commissioned and the complaints abate as people stop watching. Then begins fresh worry about the ratings.

To minimise the disruption, both the BBC and IBA have evolved the conceit of having two channels each: one with mainline entertainment (BBC 1 and ITV) and a serious, worthwhile channel that nobody watches (BBC 2 and Channel 4).

America has few such worries. There is the Public Broadcasting Service, PBS (or Channel 13) the heavyweight national network which replaces commercials with its own on-screen begging. But you can point out that it is watched by little more than 2 million households in a country of 250 million people and makes few programmes of its own.

Apart from this minor aberration American television goes for laughs and big money. There are three commercial networks – ABC, CBS and NBC – but affiliated to them are over 1200 small privately owned stations. To maximise profits, there are commercial breaks every 8 minutes. Thus even relatively serious and well-made programmes such as the news are fragmented into short sections and constantly adapted to zap into popular taste. You should know that American television turned this to advantage with the invention in the 1960s of the **magazine programme**. All American television is obsessed not only by upping the ratings but also 'maximising the audience profile'. Thus they have revitalised the advertising potential of traditional current affairs with the invention of the '**Yupdoc**' – smart, slick programmes fronted by young presenters to ensnare high-income and upwardly mobile young people.

If America salves its conscience with PBS, Japan has no such need. Although state run, the television service specialises in bad taste. There are rape scenes in prime-time drama, large helpings of pornography and game shows in which contestants eat cockroaches. In June 1985, there was even a real murder filmed and relayed on the national early evening news. The item included an interview with the freshly blood-stained killers.

Japanese television is ideal fodder for the 'social significance' approach. Despite the sex, violence and general anguish on the screen, the reported crime rate in Japan is lower than in countries where television is sternly censored. Use this factoid as necessary.

Italian television, on the other hand, mirrors society accurately insofar as it is a complete and utter muddle. In Italy there are over 800 independent stations vying for the airwaves and threatening to swamp the three state-run channels. Catholic Italian television is now approaching the bad-taste levels of Japan – the Fiat production line in Turin regularly grinds to a halt as workers tune in to the local station's most popular programme: a showcase of housewive's striptease. Faced with such competition, the state channel RAI has brightened up the news with an all-singing, all-dancing presenter.

But whatever the effect of the programmes in different countries, the medium itself can have a profoundly irrational effect. Cite the example of Ethiopia. In 1984, the government spent £3.5 million to update the television network and convert it to colour. Yet with the average Ethiopian earning only £80 a year, only one in every 1,400 people can afford any television, let alone colour.

Finally, whatever system is used, whatever the varieties of race, creed or colour, in world television one universal and immutable rule applies. Everyone watches *Dallas*.

JARGON

Saturated by jargon, some TV practitioners adopt a pose of self-conscious technical ignorance. They know perfectly well that the thing in front of them is a 'downstream-keyed digital visual effects bank' but will only refer to it as 'that funny box with knobs on'.

There are many everyday words in television language but few mean what any sane human being would think they mean. Learn some of the following and use them in the proper way: to obfuscate, disconcert and confuse.

Dog – Short for Digitally Operated Graphic. Usually appears as a programme logo to the left of a contributor's name when it is flashed on the screen. Summoned or rejected by the studio director with the commands 'dog in' or 'dog out'.

Bird – A satellite. Thus news editors describe their use of a satellite to bring in a foreign story as 'hanging a bird'. Don't confuse a **bird** with a 'heron', 'crane' or 'snipe' – these are names for different types of camera mount used in outside broadcasts.

Babies – A short set of legs. In other words a small tripod used for low-angle shots.

Real People – Television producer's description for anyone who doesn't work in television. The only exception to this rule is politicians.

Artistes – Producer's pejorative description for anyone who a) doesn't work in television, b) isn't a real person, c) isn't a politician. The term refers to actors, musicians, presenters and any other 'talent' that has to be bought in to make a programme.

Talking Head – An interviewee. 'Talking heads' are the staple of cheap television; it doesn't matter how sincere or emotional a contributor may be, all that matters to the producer is how long the interview can run without getting boring. Get a few 'good talkers' together and it's easy to fill your slot. Talking heads come in different sizes, but are most commonly seen as . . .

BCU and **MCU** – Shot sizes 'Big Close-Up' and 'Medium Close-Up'. Many directors prefer the sadistic alternatives to these phrases: instead of being asked for an '**MLS**' (Medium Long Shot) of a contributor, the cameraman is told to 'cut him at the knees'.

French Take (also known as **frenching it** or the **strawberry filter**) – The much-used technique of pretend filming and a supposedly tactful way of saving money. When an interviewee or artist has served their purpose or is found to be useless, the director uses these terms to instruct the cameraman not to waste any more expensive film. Letting the camera run on empty keeps everybody happy without the need for embarrassing explanations.

Lord Privy Seal – The belief that every word or idea must be illustrated. The term has its origins in a sixties comedy sketch by David Frost in which the parliamentary title Lord Privy Seal was illustrated by pictures of a baronet, an outside lavatory and an aquatic mammal.

Wild Tracks – Chunks of sound recorded without an accompanying picture. Mention also 'buzz tracks' and 'atmos. tracks', endless rolls of background noise which are mixed into the final film to disguise clumsy cuts and joins. 'Atmos. tracks' of bird song are also used in studios to give greater verisimilitude to the plastic tree in the cardboard garden that you're meant to believe really is outside.

FX – Additional sound effects ('FX') added to a single composite track. Favourite examples are bicycle bells, door creaks, car horns and dog barks. Because the same small selection of sound effect records is used throughout broadcasting, the same dog has been barking on films for the last twenty years.

Wallpaper – Old bits of library film haphazardly edited together to 'illustrate' drab scripts while the presenter's voice continues to drone. Watch out for the classics: 'exterior Parliament', used when anything at all is happening in politics or 'man at filling station' used whenever petrol is mentioned. As with FX, library stocks are limited so it's almost always the same man filling up the same car.

Leader – Not the person in charge – no such definite job title would be tolerated – but a strip of celluloid at the beginning of a film printed with numbers. Used to prevent films from starting **out of sync**, they are not intended to be seen on air, but often are, due to the inaccuracy of . . .

Run Cues – A pre-arranged starting signal for film or video machines usually five or ten seconds long. So in live programmes if a director forgets to run something, the presenter is left high and dry: either they have to read any remaining words very slowly or they have to waffle even more than usual until something appears.

Junctions – The place where two programmes meet.

While most producers are concerned with crafting an epic, there is a small band of renegades whose sole aim is to make creative endeavour fit into a pre-ordained schedule. 'Presentation' or 'network control' have one absolute power: if a programme over-runs, they can 'pull the plug' and take it off the air. For any producer this is the ultimate horror.

Line-Up – Studio engineers' euphemism for doing nothing. In the old days camera equipment was notoriously unreliable and had to be carefully tweaked before a recording or transmission. Modern cameras have few such problems. Even so custom and practice dictates two daily line-up periods of half-an-hour each.

Programme Development – The Producers' answer to line-up. Like 'working at home', 'preparing a treatment' or 'planning a script', this also means doing nothing.

Independent Producers – The desperate and unemployed. Willing even to undertake . . .

Access Programmes – Programmes made by public pressure groups with a producer on hand to help. Analogous to asking a legless duck to swim up Niagara, it proves that however incompetent most television producers may be, the public are infinitely worse and every bit as bitchy.

Grey Scale – 1) A testcard showing graded steps from white to black used during the adjustment of colour video cameras. 2) The hierarchy of television management.

THE BLUFFER'S GUIDES

Available now @ £1.00 each:

Accountancy
Antiques
Class
Computers
Consultancy
Golf
Hi-Fi
Hollywood
Management

Music
Paris
Philosophy
Sex
Teaching
Television
Theatre
Wine

Coming, September & October 1987:

Feminism
Jazz
Literature
Modern Art

Bluffing
Marketing
Photography
Publishing

All these books are available at your local bookshop or newsagent, or can be ordered direct from the publisher. Just tick the titles you require and fill in the form below. Prices and availability subject to change without notice.

Ravette Limited, 3 Glenside Estate, Star Road, Partridge Green, Horsham, West Sussex RH13 8RA

Please send a cheque or postal order, and allow the following for postage and packing. UK 25p for one book and 10p for each additional book ordered.

Name...

Address..

....

THE BLUFFER'S GUIDES

In preparation:

Advertising
Architecture
Astrology
Ballet
Bank Managers
Beliefs
The Body
Cinema
The Classics
Defence
Espionage
Finance
Gambling
High Society
Journalism
Law
Millionaires
Opera
Politics
Property
Psychiatry

Public Relations
Secret Societies
Selling
Ski-ing
Stocks & Shares
Travel
University
World Affairs

The Americans
The Australians
The British
The French
The Germans
The Japanese

Amsterdam
Berlin
Hong Kong
Moscow
New York